THE ART OF HUGGING

THE ART OF HUGGING

A HEARTWARMING GUIDE TO EVERYONE'S FAVORITE GESTURE OF LOVE

BRAINARD AND DELIA CAREY

Skyhorse Publishing

Skyhorse Publishing books may be purchased in bulk at special discounts for sales promotion, corporate gifts, fund-raising, or educational purposes. Special editions can also be created to specifications. For details, contact the Special Sales Department, Skyhorse Publishing, 307 West 36th Street, 11th Floor, New York, NY 10018 or info@skyhorsepublishing.com.

Skyhorse® and Skyhorse Publishing® are registered trademarks of Skyhorse Publishing, Inc.®, a Delaware corporation.

Visit our website at www.skyhorsepublishing.com.

10 9 8 7 6 5 4 3 2 1

Library of Congress Cataloging-in-Publication Data is available on file.

ISBN: 978-1-61608-714-2

Printed in China

Contents

Introduction

I will not play at tug o' war
I'd rather play at hug o' war,
Where everyone hugs
Instead of tugs.

—Shel Silverstein

Introduction

Y OU HAVE A BOOK in your hands that might change the way you interact with the world. Beware; you might suddenly get an urge to go out on the street and follow the Do-It-Yourself guide provided here and give hugs to random people as they pass. You have been warned that this could change your whole attitude towards the world, and friends might see your newfound glow and ask you what your secret is.

We launched the Free Hugs Movement in New York in 1999. As part of the culture of Free Hugs, which has grown dramatically over the last decade, including other people around the world contributing with videos, stickers, and T-shirts, we have continued to give hugs for our personal benefit as well as the smiles it generates in everyone we hug.

We are living in a culture that is increasingly complex, with our use of social media creating more ways to connect with people electronically than ever. We have an infinite appetite, it seems, for playing with keyboards and touch pads and pixels. The gesture of the hug rose dramatically in this culture, because, after all, we still need touch, we need kindness, we need to be needed.

This is a book of life. It explains how to carry a sign into the world and spread joy and life everywhere. Like the beautiful shining star that you are, you will be recognized by all of those wanting to see the same in themselves. Be brave, be bold, and make your mark in this world by sharing your beautiful spirit with everyone.

The History and Art of a Simple Gesture

Every day you should reach out and touch someone. People love a warm hug, or just a friendly pat on the back.
—Maya Angelou

Chapter One

The History and Art of a Simple Gesture

A HUG IS ONE OF the most simple and unadorned gestures of affection, but is meant to communicate a specific feeling or idea, such as forgiveness, in a wordless, intimate way. It is a gesture that is visible in art throughout history, and one that continues to create sentimental feelings in media from greeting cards to viral videos. One area of hugging not so explored is the research that shows it is even good for your health. But before we talk about the less obvious benefits of this heartwarming gesture, let's ask the simplest question: why are we interested in the humble hug?

We are living in a world that is fully wired, getting ready for the oncoming tide of electronic and new technology to help us communicate. In a time when you can "poke" a friend through the internet and read someone's expression from halfway around the world, the hug is one of those rare holdouts that continues to be valuable despite our changing world. A hug is one of the most primal gestures of peace and affection.

We are all interested in this idea and feeling, because we want a hug on the most basic level. We all want a connection with other people, whether it's intimate or platonic. Admitting that we want a hug is a hurdle in itself, but the act of receiving one or giving one is satisfying in a physical and emotional way that perhaps has the ability to truly change the world. By "changing the world," we don't mean that the humble hug can end hunger or war, only that it can introduce more peace into our daily lives.

Who would argue against that? It has always been at the very least a symbol of forgiveness and reconciliation, because both parties are displaying that they are unarmed and without malicious intent. A hug reveals a person's vulnerability, and their openness to affection. Therein lies its beauty. Of course, there could be deceptive hugs, just as one can do just about anything insincerely, but in this book, we are

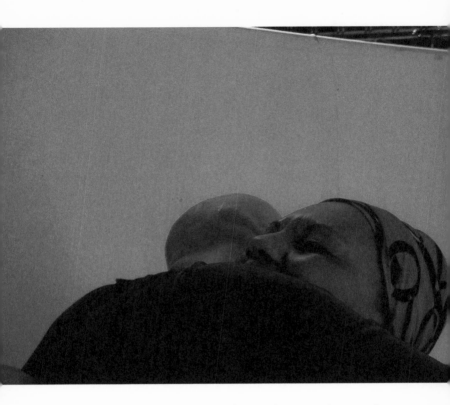

concerned with the genuine hug, the one that makes everyone smile.

You will also find a manual here on how to give out free hugs in your neighborhood, if you wish. Not only is it an exhilarating activity to do on a beau-

tiful afternoon, but it can also be a fundraiser for your local cause by getting people to sponsor hugs in advance.

{ THE FORGIVING HUG }

One meaning of the hug is forgiveness. The image of two known enemies hugging in reconciliation is one that can truly move you to tears. Can you think of any images like that you might already know? I am sure you have seen some, like the unlikely friendship that can come at the end of a bitter battle. After the riots in Los Angeles in the '90s after the Rodney King beating, a truck driver was pulled from his truck and beaten by bystanders. When that went to trial, at the end was an image of the truck driver hugging one of the people that had beaten him. In 1993, Fulbright Scholar Amy Biehl was brutally murdered amidst the rising violence of apartheid. It was the type of death that could have sparked another wave of violence, but incredibly, the lasting image that emerged from the Amy Biehl tragedy was that of her parents embracing her murderers in forgiveness. In fact, her father, Peter Biehl, spoke the following words regarding the pardon of her killers:

>+ +<

"The most important vehicle of reconciliation is open and honest dialogue ... we are here to reconcile a human life which was taken without an opportunity for dialogue. When we are finished with this process we must move forward with linked arms."

>+ +<

The actions of the Biehl family perhaps set a standard to which most of us cannot hope to rise, but it's an easier task to move through the world with linked arms, as Peter Biehl suggests, and to embrace the art of the embrace. That is because hugging in itself is so disarming that it is almost an instant gesture of being forgiven, blessed, comforted, or nurtured. The act itself doesn't have the power to help build a new nation or hold the attention of the world, but the intention behind it, the courage to forgive, can move mountains.

THE PROTECTIVE HUG

A protective hug is a powerful image. These are the kind of hugs that a mother or father would give a child to protect it from crying more. It is perhaps the first hug we experience, the hug of complete protection, the sense of being entirely safe. Parents often embrace their infants, but even the way an infant is held could be considered a hug, and perhaps the most powerful one in the world. When we first had a child, we had a choice in how we would train him

to go to sleep on his own. One method of teaching a child to fall asleep asks the parents not to go to the infant's room or crib when he or she is crying. The child learns that you will come back eventually and calms down. The other method for putting your child to sleep is more labor-intensive—you just pick up your child whenever it is crying and hold it until it stops and falls asleep again. Eventually the child will sleep longer and longer that way. We chose to do the latter, and pick up our child whenever he cried, an experience that is echoed across the world. For many people, the sense of being in a parent's embrace is one of our first memories.

As children, we are also held or hugged by other people, perhaps relatives and close friends. All of these embraces are protective embraces. With an infant, everyone is careful to support its head and body and keep it clear of sharp objects. There is an instinct in even the most child-averse of adults to protect a smaller body, and keep it safe. The protective hug is not limited to parents and their children, but extends to anyone who holds affection for another person, anyone who would put themselves in harm's way to keep someone else safe.

THE HUG IN WARTIME

We also see the gesture in war, like a soldier covering another soldier in battle, or perhaps a soldier

embracing one or more members of a family or group to protect them from raining debris that could hurt them. In war photographs, we see images of soldiers embracing each other for victory and also to console grieving comrades after troop fatalities. The protective embrace in war or in a violent scene is often one of martyrdom, where the protector is shot or killed in place of the person being protected. In that case, the hug is like becoming a human shield. More than just an emotional gesture, it is also the ultimate sacrifice.

Embraces in war are not always about death. They live in the camaraderie of weary soldiers after a long tour, in the civilians of a war-torn nation breathing a sigh of relief when the fighting is done, in the comfort of a veteran returning home to a family he or she may not have seen for years. In war, which is often party to the lowest conditions humanity has to offer in terms of brutality and bloodshed, a simple touch can be the most powerful of all. Writing for the *New Yorker* about the so-called "mercy dogs" of World War I, who would range the field after a battle, providing not only first aid and water to the wounded, but also the simple comfort and touch of another living being to the dying, Susan Orlean puts it best when she says that "nothing will ever be better, or more perfect, than that."

THE LAST EMBRACE

No matter your spiritual inclination, letting go of a loved one can be one of the hardest things you'll ever have to do. In the face of the loss of the physical body, the need for touch is natural. The eerily preserved ruins of Pompeii show the last embraces of friends, of husband and wife, of mother and child. To receive as much as possible, one last time, from the person you love seems to be what a final hug is all about. It is a memory that is being consciously created. When the hug lasts for too long, or perhaps even when the people hugging are pulled apart after a hug that doesn't want to end, it is as though that hug will let us carry the person we love with us.

THE JOYOUS HUG

The hug of joy can manifest in a situation as intimate and simple as a goodnight kiss or one as epic as the toppling of a dictatorship. You can probably see one in your mind already. A contestant on a game show unexpectedly wins the grand prize and begins hugging everyone around. When New Year's Eve is celebrated around the world, the strike of the clock sets off an outpouring of hugs and embraces.

With major sports victories, the teammates embrace each other in ecstatic excitement over the win. For anyone who has been a fan, who has invested any part of themselves in the fate of an athletic team, or a movie during awards season, or even just a potato sack race at a family picnic, that moment of weightless euphoria is familiar. It is a joy that is almost hysterical, pouring out from the body to seek release and celebration even with strangers around them. It is done with abandon, without being conscious of what is happening. These moments of universality, of human contact, should be treasured. A hug like this can be given to almost anyone.

⟨ THE BEAR HUG ⟩

The term "bear hug" is used to mean a very big or powerful hug, or even an affectionate one, as in, "come

here, I am going to give you a bear hug!" It may also refer to the size of the person giving the hug. If you are taller, embracing someone significantly shorter can feel like a bear hug to that person, because your arms can completely wrap around them in a way that feels like a big bear is hugging a smaller one. This type of hug might appear cartoonish, but its outlandish enthusiasm is just an expression of joy and affection.

HUGS ON THE STREET

There are several subtle but clear distinctions in hugs that are given out casually. If you give out free hugs on the street and are simply opening your arms to people, there are several ways you might find yourself getting or giving hugs that might surprise you. Here are a few of them.

THE HANDSHAKE

Yes, some people will come up to you and shake your hand. It may not seem like a hug, but it's just as affectionate. It is a gesture of introduction and openness—just think of it as your hands hugging! So don't hesitate to take a hand as a substitute for a hug, because it will probably generate as many smiles.

THE PAT

This is a hug where either you or the person you are hugging begins to pat your back or rub it in a circular direction while you are giving a hug. Don't worry about feeling self-conscious! It's a natural comforting gesture and implies intimacy between the huggers.

THE LONG HOLD

Everyone has experienced this at least once. In an embrace, the person you are hugging does not let go when you do. This could be a sign of simply wanting more, or it could mask something deeper at work, such as someone who is wounded or hurt for instance. It's a delicate situation, but don't be too quick to let go! Hugging shouldn't be one-sided, but you shouldn't deprive someone of comfort, either. Enjoy the embrace!

THE SPIN

An experience that literally lifts you off your feet! If you are the one spinning, it means you hug, lean back, lift the other person, and spin around or back and forth. It is the kind of hug you see when a soldier comes home or a loved one is saved from something. It might be the hug you give your spouse after getting married. This is the hug of unbridled joy, and it's wonderful to watch.

THE JUMP

Sometimes a hug is so exuberant that it can't be contained on the ground! Of course, you have to be strong enough to support the weight of a person on you, but it is a version of the hug that is often seen in movies and media, dramatic to the max. If you are the one jumping, it feels like you're dipping back into a warm childhood memory.

THE SELF-HUG

That's right—you can create a hug with an army of one! That may seem a bit crazy, but in truth, it only takes one person to give a hug. You can hug yourself. It is simple, and you can do it when you are alone, if you like. Stop reading this book and give yourself a hug. It can be a short one, but just try it, and while you are doing it, close your eyes and compliment yourself. Try it now.

THE CYBER-HUG

Although it may seem impersonal, sending someone a hug online by just saying so conveys part of the feeling. A simple sign-off can brighten some-

one's day. There are even online games that allow you to virtually hug someone else; they connect families and friends from across the world in a way that was impossible not so long ago. From love letters and gifts in centuries past to the newest streaming technology today, hugs delivered from afar are just as important.

THE GROUP HUG

The group hug is both therapeutic and joyous, often delivered at the end of a long shared project or victory. It can be a wonderful icebreaker or a sweet farewell to a great team. Despite its cheesy reputation, the group hug can create an instant physical bond in a group. It can be done with as few as three people, but a dozen (or more!) is even better!

THE SHOULDER HUG

This is the red carpet hug that tends to show off each participant to his or her best advantage. You'll see it on television, with the people facing the camera, arms around each other's shoulders. It's designed to be seen by a third person or camera. Show off your affection to the world!

SIGNING A HUG

With both hands, cross your arms and with curved hands grab your biceps. It looks like you are hugging yourself. If you do it once, it is the verb "to give a hug," and if you repeat it twice, it is either the noun form of a hug, or it can mean the action of hugging. If you twist a little bit while doing this for emphasis, it means an extended hug, or a long one. This is how you hug through American Sign Language. It is said that deaf people hug more than hearing Americans do. For the deaf, eye contact is very important, and hugging has a deeper meaning than it might to your average person.

In *Reading Between the Signs*, Anna Mindess writes that deaf people not only hug more people from a wider circle than hearing people do, but that their hugs tend to have more body contact, to the point where they might make fun of hearing friends for their "weak" hugs. For the deaf, a hug is something that is taught to children early on, with an established protocol. There is a "right moment" to hug, usually right after saying "hello." But if the moment passes due to distraction, then it will not occur again until parting. The parting

hug, or good-bye hug, is particularly different in deaf culture, and often misunderstood by the hearing. It is an eloquent gesture that communicates all the usual verbal niceties that the hearing use when bidding someone farewell. In the deaf community, the hug is a powerful language all its own.

THE AUTOMATIC HUG

It would seem that a hug is an intrinsically organic gesture that could never be replaced by a machine, but in 1965, a hug machine was invented. It was and still is a very important tool. The machine was the brainchild of Temple Grandin, an autistic child growing up on her aunt's farm in Wisconsin. She noticed that when the cows were getting medicine or shots for disease prevention, they were put in a squeeze chute, and some seemed to calm down right away. As a child living with autism and related symptoms, she was uncomfortable and overstimulated with a hug from a person, but she also craved what is called "pressure stimulation," which calmed and relaxed her. She invented what is known as the hug machine or squeeze box. It is made out of two hinged side-boards, each four by three feet (120 cm by 90 cm) with thick soft padding, which form a V-shape, with a complex control box at one end and heavy-duty tubes leading to an air compressor. The user lies or squats between the side-boards, for as long or short a period as desired. Using pressure exerted by the air compressor and controlled by the user, the side-boards apply deep pressure stimulation evenly across the lateral parts of the body.

The hug machine shows us that the need to be held, to feel safe, is a primal urge that isn't even limited to human beings. It is a universal urge that links us all together on both the physiological and emotional levels. The machine itself is still in use in therapy practices, primarily as a relaxing technique for those with autism and autism-spectrum disorders. Grandin published significant research in the *American Journal of Occupational Therapy* about the machine's utility in reducing tension. When *Time* magazine asked her in 2010 if she still used it, she shook her head, "I'm into hugging people now."

CHAPTER TWO

Amma, the Hugging Saint

We need four hugs a day for survival. We need eight hugs a day for maintenance. We need twelve hugs a day for growth.

—Virginia Satir

Amma, the Hugging Saint

HUGGING IS NOT ONLY a prosaic gesture, but one that can be used as a form of worship. Born in India, Amma gives hugs for over eight hours at a time, and has raised money for schools and hospitals. Like a new Mother Teresa, her focus is on helping those who suffer. Born Sudhamani at birth, it is said that she came into this world not crying as babies usually do, but smiling while looking happy and content. It was the beginning of her journey to bring bliss and joy to the world. Sudhamani spent years of her childhood and adolescence totally immersed in intense spiritual practices that would bring her the knowledge and strength to present her real self to the world. Even as a very young child, she could often be found deeply absorbed in meditation, totally submerged in a higher world. She started composing devotional songs with deep mystical insight by the age of five. Another special quality that was clearly manifest in her from this tender age was her compassion and love toward her fellow human beings.

Though only a child, Sudhamani did whatever was in her hands to ease the suffering of her elderly neighbors. She bathed them, washed their clothes, and even brought them food and clothing from her own home. This habit that she formed of giving away things from her family's house got her into big trouble. However, no amount of physical abuse or punishment could stop the big expression of her inborn compassionate being. She later said, "An unbroken stream of love flows from me towards all beings in the cosmos. That is my inborn nature."

The Amritapuri Ashram in India was the first spiritual center that was established by Amma. She lives there today along with more than two thousand residents who come from all over the world. Amma has established spiritual centers across the globe; every single one of these centers provides an ideal environment to meditate and perform selfless

service, supporting Amma's innumerable humanitarian activities.

We first heard about Amma, the hugging saint, when we were living in New York's East Village in 2001. She was coming to New York for a few days and was in an auditorium in midtown Manhattan, giving out hugs. We both arrived early, before 9 a.m., and there was not only a line to see her, but you had to get a number just to get in line. When we looked down at the number on our tickets, it was over a thousand. The auditorium was over twenty-thousand square feet with a stage at one end. And there was Amma, simply sitting on the floor. A small exhibit and tables full of material about her charitable efforts in India occupied our time while we waited. There we learned about her poverty-stricken childhood and how hard she'd worked to achieve her international presence. It was incredible to see all the relief work she was doing, and the organization she started. But we were there for a hug.

When our number came up, we were told to get on our knees when we were within fifteen minutes of seeing her. It was certainly a big build-up as we waited. There were assistants all around her, dressed in white, explaining how to approach her on your knees. When we finally came up to her, she was sitting on a low chair, leaning forward, and as you walked on your knees to her, she pulled in your head and shoulders, so you were being held against her chest, and her arms were on your back and head. If you tried to hug her by reaching around her, one of the assistants would take your hands off of her and show you that your hands must be at your sides. As you laid your head against her chest, she would recite a soft prayer that echoed in the safe space.

It was not at all the type of hug you get from a close friend—more like the way a mother might embrace a child. The hush of the huge crowd and the size of the auditorium gave the experience a holy air, like her touch was a blessing. Her mission is to help all those who suffer, and many of her followers feel that being in her presence is purifying and healing. Because she gives hugs for hours on end, her stamina and person seem almost otherworldly. It is that endurance that gives her the magnetism people call saintly.

Her hugs are not just physical, but also powerful in the spiritual realm. The success of her darshan, or her vision, is that people have come to view her hugs as healing and powerful. Her followers seek her hoping to achieve health and long life. In India, a healing from Amma may not have an equivalent in the United States, because the culture here is so different. The American craving for yoga, meditation, and other forms of Eastern spirituality has certainly fed the fascination for Amma's advice, but

the force and truth of her charity have a universal draw. There are new ways of healing all the time, and the free hugs movement is, arguably, a new spirituality in very different clothes.

We recently met a devotee of Amma and asked him about his experience with her. An American chef at a restaurant in New York, he said that he has seen Amma several times, and when we walked into his kitchen in the restaurant, he had a picture of her above his working area. A second picture was in the locket around his neck. In glowing terms, he talked of Amma as a living saint who has personally healed him. He told us a story about a time in his life when he was going through a great transition. While racked with uncertainty in the middle of this situation, he said he felt a light touch on his shoulder, so distinct that he turned around, but no one was there. Yet he sensed that it was Amma's presence there, calming him, allowing him to go forward with his life. Regardless of whether or not you believe in the spiritual aspect of his story, it's undeniable that Amma's message had inspired him and improved his life. He credits Amma with that change and looks at her image daily in devotion to her healing abilities.

Amma lives to spread her message all around the world. She does not teach anything that she herself does not practice. Living in a state of serenity, Amma hugs thousands of people day after day, helping them find a way to happiness, giving them her divine knowledge, and offering complete solace to all that come for help. We are not asking anyone to take the healing hug as a full-time job, or turn it into an international charity, but her story should remind us that even a few minutes spent in happiness can influence our lives. If we could just make a little bit of an effort to try to commit ourselves to a discipline of being kind, of giving out hugs, every day, then we too could make a change.

Even if we just give one hug a day, to our relatives, pets, friends, somebody in the store, at work, even just to ourselves in a blue moment, we can enact a small shift that tilts the world for the better. This way we can become closer to ourselves. A hug is an act of kindness that is as spiritual as you want it to be. It is both spontaneous and an act that can benefit from discipline. You can write down how many hugs you give in a week, a month, or a year, or just push yourself out of your own comfort zone occasionally and reach out to another person. Whether your goal is a number or just a better state of mind, you will grow.

CHAPTER THREE

Free Hugs, Our Story

A hug is like a boomerang—you get it back right away.

—Bil Keane

Free Hugs, Our Story

W E MET IN THE East Village in the winter of 1998. We were both artists and began living together in a small storefront on East 10th Street. Our relationship turned into an art collaborative that would soon make artwork and performances for museums around the world, but one of our favorite collaborations is still the free hug movement.

When we met, we had both recently been divorced and were in our early twenties, looking for something new. Delia had moved to New York City from her native country, Spain, and Brainard had moved from a small island off the coast of Rhode Island. We were both in a runway fashion show as models, but not

because that is what we did, but because we were artists who had been asked to collaborate with the designer. Have you ever had that nightmare where you realize you're naked in front of a crowd? Imagine that being your first date!

We created the role of Adam and Eve, and decided to bare it all as a strong statement about clothes. It was a strange way to meet, to stand next to someone who is completely naked and work on how you will walk and act. However, like any performance, we got used to the idea, and enjoyed the dress rehearsals for the show. After several rehearsals, we got to know each other much better, but it would be months before we kissed one another. When the runway show took place, it was like a wonderful nightmare, to be so vulnerable in front of such a huge crowd, but it was also incredibly freeing. When you have nothing to hide, you have nothing to lose. We were able to blend with each other both spiritually and physically. In opening ourselves up to something new, we both found love.

One thing led to another, and a kiss goodbye became something much deeper, and just a few months after we started dating, we were married at

the Angel Orensanz Foundation. It is housed in the oldest synagogue in New York City, a Lower East Side landmark, and completely self-sustaining thanks to its status as one of New York City's most popular event venues. The Foundation maintains its role in the Lower East Side art community by providing an exhibition space at the lower level of the building. We were the quintessential free spirits who hadn't hesitated when something felt right. Though some of our friends almost doubted how quickly we fell in love, we never did. We had this tremendous feeling of love, not only for each other, but for others; we were glowing and we wanted to convey what we were feeling to the world. Like Amma, we wanted to turn that peace outwards.

In the storefront on East 10th Street, we were sharing art and music with our circle of friends. As artists, we began thinking about ways to tell the world something that is wordless and personal: the love between two people. We wanted to reach out in any way possible. The first idea was to wash feet. It crossed a boundary that in the modern era many people have learned not to broach. It was a loving expression, an intimate one, to share with strangers.

We simply put a sandwich board sign out on the street and began waiting for people to come in. No donations, no fuss.

People got curious. Those who were passing by would come in and ask us what was going on. The process was simple—we had a basin of water and fresh towels and used liquid soap. We had struck out with little idea as to what we could expect, but what we got was wonderful. People came in and stayed and asked questions and talked to us. They could see we were in love, and the feeling of it all made for conversation topics about giving and receiving, relationships and love. A small community was formed through all the visitors that we came to know. We had weekly dinners where we invited friends over to eat. We were making new friends and they accepted us and our love, and the things we were doing together. We had achieved our goal and more, and we were very happy and thought about our next steps. We wanted to take it out into the world even more and go to museums and galleries with it, because as artists, we wanted to share an experience we had enjoyed creating.

We decided to expand our little storefront. To our menu of free services, we added hugs, bandages,

and money. The biggest letters of all, however, were the ones that read FREE HUGS.

In September of that year, we had a show at a small gallery in Brooklyn called Rotunda, and it was featured in the *New York Times*. In that gallery we gave out foot-washings, hugs, and bandages for non-visible wounds. The bandages were something people had never seen before. We would ask people if they wanted a bandage for a visible or non-visible wound. Sometimes they would say to put one on their forehead for a headache or on their stomach to help them with stomachache.

Then after applying it, we would kiss the band-aid the way a mother might, to help whatever discomfort they were feeling, to heal. We certainly didn't claim sainthood, but it was at times very revealing and quite emotional. One woman asked us to put a bandage low on her stomach, her hand falling over her womb. She had been trying to have a child for a long time, with no success. To her, the bandage was a wish, or a prayer, to have the child she wanted. Though we promised no miracles, when we saw her again a year later at the museum, she was pregnant! Call it luck or divine wisdom or just good faith, but we like to think we at least brightened up her hope that day she first walked in.

We continued working out of our storefront, and eventually a curator from a museum in New York, PS1/MoMA, which is the Museum of Modern Art's more ambitious outpost, came by and asked us to be in their Greater New York Show, which we gladly accepted. There we gave out over 600 hugs in less than five hours. It was a great success, and in the art world, people loved it. The audience members who were just trying to look at art found us, and responded in a very open and kind way. It had changed the way they perceived the museum experience. Instead of trying to understand art and pick their favorites, they were led into an experience that made them look at art and the role of museums differently. That show changed the way we saw the whole act of giving out hugs.

The hugs were no longer a storefront whim that had drawn a quirky community. They were now an art experience. People referred to it as a performance, and of course it was and it wasn't. For museum-goers, it was performance art, but there was no stage, and the audience was performing as much as we were. That made it a new kind of performance art, one that wasn't easy to define. Because we were in a museum,

it also made it art with a capital A. It seemed new to people, and was brimming with a sense of fun and intimacy. Curators and writers began asking us more questions about how and why we were doing this, and they also brought their own agenda and thoughts to the conversation.

The idea of "relational aesthetics" was revived in the critical discussion of the exhibit. It traced its roots back to the 1960s group Fluxus, which included conceptual performances by artists like Yoko Ono. While we knew the art world well, this particular work was about the community around us, wherever we were, and not exclusively for the art world and its patrons. However, we loved that this simple gesture could inspire a critical conversation as easily as it could a smile.

Back at our storefront, we began taking pictures and video taping many of those experiences. Since it was the East Village, all kinds of people came through. On one occasion, the performance artist Karen Finley dropped by. She was, then and now, infamous for her aggressive performances and volatile personality. Karen Finley was practically a professional provocateur. She didn't back down, took

no prisoners. We had no idea what to expect, but we were already videotaping when she came in. She received her hug and foot-washing. After her feet had been hand-dried with a towel, we asked her the same questions we asked everyone that came in. *Who are we? What do we do?*

Everyone had different answers, but Karen Finley was almost stumped. She said we were artists, practicing their art. *What do we do?* A healing of some kind, she responded, people who offered comfort. She was positively tamed. Relaxed, genuinely thankful, and humbled.

Two years later we were still giving out hugs, Delia was pregnant with our child, and we were very happy living in New York City. As artists, we were beginning a whole new life, we were having a child, and we wanted to find a way to continue giving hugs without compromising ourselves. We knew a child would take a lot of energy, time, and money, and we wanted to remain artists, not become worker bees! That was in 2000, before the age of YouTube, so we started sending out DVDs to museums and campaigning to expand what we were doing.

The hugs became a national news story when we were asked to be in a prestigious art show, the Whitney Biennial, in New York. In the museum, we gave out hugs, and were interviewed on *Good Morning America*. It was a shocking and exciting time. Our lives were changing fast as we were reviewed by some of the top critics in the art world at the time, such as Arthur Danto. The Biennial was in 2002; in the wake of 9/11, an exhibit such as ours served as a source of public comfort for those who sought it. The hugs, sprung from something so simple, so primal, made people question the line between instinct and art, performance and nature. Most of all, it was cinematic, and people wanted to see more. We made our own hugging video that was shown in the museum, and soon that became the video that many people associated with the beginning of the Free Hug movement, which was soon to come.

Shiva was born the very first day of the year in 2001. It felt like all the stars were aligning for us. Besides being in love and having a beautiful baby, we were spending most of our time giving away hugs and celebrating life. It was a privilege to live in such serenity, and we tried to shape ourselves to be equal to such an existence. Even today, we do not drink or smoke; we eat raw foods; and we meditate and visualize regularly. Did that all play a major role? Maybe. We had taken that spark of love and shared it with the world.

It wasn't just art, but also a service to the community. Thinking of hugs as a service defines the concept rather neatly, because you literally get what you are giving. As the saying goes, what you put out, comes back to you. In this case, that law may have been at work, because giving out hugs tends to bring a lot to you. In our case, things just got better, and why shouldn't they have? We were, and are, happy! The publicity opened up more opportunities for us in the art world. We were able to travel the world, sharing our affection wherever we went. We had built a community, a career, a warm world in which our child could grow up.

And it all started with little more than a hug.

Free Hugs Go Viral

CHAPTER FOUR

Free Hugs Go Viral

THE FREE HUGS CONTINUED out of our storefront on East 10th Street, four days a week, every week, for the years 1999 to 2006. After that we decided to focus more on traveling to give away hugs and create other situations where the viewer is intimately involved. In those years at the beginning of the millennium, there was a community in the East Village that was building around our activities, and many conversations took place within our storefront. We had curators come by, as well as the media, and artists, and others who also asked us how to do the same. In an informal way, we told them to go out on the streets and simply give away hugs with a sign or whatever they wanted. Several friends did it in the neighborhood, and the word began to spread, especially after the news coverage from the

Whitney Museum and the video we made of us giving out hugs. We also started giving out hugs in Union Square in NYC, with a sign, and began to do it all over the city in different places. Free hugs were about to take the world by storm.

JONATHAN LITTMAN

In May of 2004, a man named Jonathan Littman began giving out hugs in Washington Square Park. He gave them out every Sunday beneath a sign proudly labeled FREE HUGS. He also traveled to Germany and gave out hugs there as well. A business man with a natural gregariousness to him, he used generosity as a way to connect more with the people around him.

JUAN MANN

A month later, in June of 2004, Juan Mann gave out hugs for the first time with a sign in Sydney, Australia, in the same way that Jonathan Littman had done it and the same way we had done it. But Juan had something even more powerful than the *New York Times:* viral video. The band Sick Puppies created a

Juan Mann

music video out of his travels that was immediately addictive. The story began to spread.

Juan Mann reached his decision about free hugs in the simplest and most poignant of ways. He decided to give out hugs because he wanted to receive them. No psychoanalysis, no critical theory. Just a desire to reach out and be comforted. That's a great motivation, isn't it? He made a sign, went out into the street, and began waiting for people to give him hugs. YouTube was coming into prominence at the same time, and the two rose together. The video traveled the world instantly, and people began dispensing hugs of their own. Though Juan retired from the movement in 2009, it continues to thrive without him.

We continued to give away hugs, and created immersive installations for the art world, but when people recognized us from the hugs video, we were asked all about it and explained what it meant to us and why it began. The "Free Hug" movement, as it is known, became our most famous action, and to this day we travel to art biennials and museums as well as the streets and continue to give away hugs.

Though it's been years, it's a movement that's really just begun. Millions of people watched Juan Mann and others perform this beautifully simple and

charitable deed, and others followed across the globe. All over the world people are giving out hugs on the street and at home. *The Art of Hugging* will show you that it's not only a wonderful way to have fun and spread joy, but also a powerful force for charity and fundraising.

It's no surprise that the free hug movement took the globe by storm.

After all, hugging is one of the most natural things in the world!

CHAPTER FIVE

Hugs Are Healthy

Everybody needs a hug. It changes your metabolism.

—Leo Buscaglia

Hugs Are Healthy

DID YOU KNOW THE giving and receiving of hugs is good for everything from stress to blood pressure and general immune building response?

It may seem like common sense, the idea that a hug can be healthy, but if we look more carefully at research that has been done, it's more than just wishful thinking. As children, we all know when any of life's difficulties arise, from a cut or bruise to a bully's taunts, the embrace of a mother is more than comforting; it is a destination that we can count on. It heals quite literally, and has an immediate effect upon us for the better. As adults we also know this, but may unconsciously resist it. To find out if you are resisting, try this technique with your partner or someone you live with. Make a pact that whenever you get angry or upset, the other person will quickly open their

arms in the gesture to receive and give a hug. That means if you, or the person you are living with, gets upset, it is the other person's job to open their arms and wait for an embrace. What you may find while doing this exercise is curious. When you are angry or upset, and you begin to rant or rave, and the person near you offers a hug, do you resist it? Most people do for some reason. Even though it is just like a mother's gesture, as adults we may feel we have to carry the burden on our own, or worse, we want to feel sorry for ourselves.

No matter what the reason might be, if you are resisting a hug when you need it most, you might want to consider crossing that threshold and seeing what happens. That means taking the hug from your partner, even if you are not ready. What can happen is like magic—all your troubles slowly melt away in an embrace. If they don't melt away, then hold on, it is not time to let go.

RESEARCH ON THE HEALTH OF HUGS

Two researchers from the Department of Psychiatry at the University of North Carolina at Chapel Hill conducted a study to determine if the warmth and closeness of a hug can actually make a difference in physiological terms. Can it lower blood pressure and help to ease the onslaught of challenges to our body on a daily basis? Their research shows that, yes, in fact it can do just that and more.

In the study, two groups of adults who were either married or had been living together were chosen. They were divided into two groups. In group one, there were 100 adults who were told to hold hands for at least ten minutes while viewing a pleasant video. After the video they were to hug for twenty seconds. In group two, there were 85 adults who were told not to do anything during that time, to just sit quietly. When that was done, all participants were asked to stand up and give a short description of something that irritated or angered them. Then they all had their blood pressure and heart rate tested. In the group of non-huggers, their heart rate and blood pressure were significantly higher than the huggers, and women seemed to be affected even more than men.

Another study focused on the varying levels of oxytocin in the blood. At the 2004 annual meeting of the American Psychosomatic Society, results from a new study involving 76 adults who were either married or in long-term cohabitating relationships were presented. In that study, partners or spouses who described their relationship as happy had significantly higher levels of oxytocin compared with duos who described themselves as unhappy. Each couple was asked to converse privately for five minutes regarding some circumstances that drew them closer to one another, then to watch a romantic video together and to hug each other. During these warm contacts, women experienced significantly higher levels of oxytocin, and lower blood pressure compared to men. It is possible that oxytocin triggers physiological changes that help to protect the emotional stability of women, and that their so-called "nesting" tendencies benefit not only their mates and offspring, but also themselves.

THE HEART

Perhaps we don't need scientists to tell us that a hug is healthy, but in this case, with measurable levels of oxytocin and the drop in blood pressure, we have the evidence that it is more than just a warm feeling or a sense of happiness. Real change is happening inside our bodies that might even save our lives, because we are talking about the health of the heart.

These studies also are saying that hugging will have an effect on stress levels in our body. Blood pressure, heart rate, and oxytocin levels are all related to stress. Meditation and exercise are proven to work as remedies, but what about a simple hug? In fact, hugs offer us a way to be more social and connect with our lovers and friends on a deeper level. Have you ever had a full twenty-second hug? Perhaps when you were a child or had a recent good cry with a friend and you held on, but it is rare for most people. When we give hugs in public or in our studio as part of Free Hugs, the hugs do not usually last that long—from one to five seconds at the most. In your own home, it could be different, and you can experiment with longer hugs, holding one another and knowing that your heart and your health are being protected.

If you take this approach to giving hugs, it becomes more than just a fun activity; it is truly a healthy one that has benefits for everyone. Imagine going to the doctor's office and getting a hug. If it was normal to get hugs like that all the time, perhaps we would be a much healthier culture. In Malcom Gladwell's *The*

Outliers, he cites a study done in a small town about the health of the inhabitants decades ago. At that time there was virtually no heart disease in the town, even though they were consuming plenty of fats and alcohol, both on the list of the usual suspects.

The doctors were stumped as to what caused the discrepancy. Gladwell proposes that it was the entire culture of the town that had affected the change. Decades before, in a less fractured world, everyone helped each other; those who had less money were supported by those who had more. They were tight-knit, affectionate, and comfortable with one another. It was a recipe for happiness that had powerful physiological effects. If a light feeling of happiness and community can have that powerful effect on heart disease, isn't it possible that hugs could do the same? The proof seems to be there, so perhaps giving out hugs and spreading the message to others could do the same, and really could help save the world. Why not?

More large companies are offering their employees a gym to exercise in, and many require that they go to the gym as part of their work day. The reason is that when employees are healthier, they tend to produce

more—they take less sick days, and the work environment becomes more inspiring. Major companies like Apple, Google, and Facebook have used techniques like this to insure that their employees remain happy and loyal as well as productive. We imagine that receiving and giving hugs could be an important part of the mix, and might in general improve the well-being of everyone.

A DAILY PRACTICE

Here is a practice you can do daily to stay healthy with hugs. Set aside a time once a day, every day, when you can devote twenty seconds to this practice. It could be first thing in the morning or just before bed. Hug your friend, family member, pet, or even a stuffed animal or yourself for a full twenty seconds. That may not seem like much time, but for a hug, it can do a world of good.

CHAPTER SIX

Virtual Hugs

Did you know that if you visualize, you
can actually hug on the phone?
—Shelly Long

CHAPTER SIX

Virtual Hugs

WHILE THE SOCIAL NETWORKS do not replace gestures like the hug, they share some of the same goals: friends and community.

If you are using a service like Skype that allows you to videoconference with anyone in the world, you could give and receive a hug that way. Think of it—you are watching a family member or friend on a computer screen, and you are talking in real time about recent news, and then you open your arms to give and receive a hug. Though the physical contact is not there, the important part—the intention, the connection—is there. There are many types of virtual hugs, but the Skype hug is one of the most effective. In August of 2009, we decided to give a hug every day to a friend on Skype. We emailed people to tell them in advance that we were going to videoconference with them and give them a hug. Everyone loved the idea, and once a day we met someone on Skype and with our arms wide open in the universal gesture.

Though there was nothing physical about it, we always ended up laughing and smiling, and it felt like a hug in the sense that it made us all happier and focused on one another. Our goal was to do it every day for a month, which we did. But because we were on Skype so much, something else happened. We began getting messages from people we had hugged. *Hi, I could use a quick hug, are you available?* Of course we connected and gave them one. We imagined it as a once-a-day exercise, but it quickly grew, and we began giving out several hugs every time we signed into Skype! Another community was building, and people were doing it with their friends, too. The next time you are on Skype, try it! You never know what will happen, but it shows us that hugs can be effective in many different forms.

PHONE HUG

It could even happen on the phone. Have you ever talked to someone on the phone and said something like "I am sending you a hug?" If you have, or at least realize that it is possible to do that, then it is another form of a virtual hug. It is an audio hug, so to speak. By telling someone they are getting a hug, it carries much of the weight of the real gesture of the hug. Think of all the phone sex out there. If that works, why wouldn't telling someone you are giving them a hug be the same? Get descriptive, be romantic when appropriate, and share the joy of it all.

FACEBOOK, GOOGLE PLUS, TWITTER, ET AL.

You can do the same on social networks like Face-book and Google Plus. If you are giving out hugs, and make a video, you can send that hug out into the world. However, there are features of Facebook that make it unique in sharing. New games and apps spring up every day. For every "poke," there's also a "hug." It's fun, quick, and casual. You can let someone know you're thinking of them in just an instant. It's the new greeting card.

The concept of sharing has taken on a whole new meaning in the digital era. While there are certainly the risks of privacy invasion and careless divulging, we also have the power to reach a much larger audience than ever before. Your virtual hugs can reach millions more than your physical ones. When you send out a hug in words, it will likely be shared. No matter what platform you're on, some of the most shared posts are ones that spread happiness. The next time you post or Tweet, curb your embarrassment, and think about throwing out an offer for a hug, or simply a "how are you?" No matter how fickle and moody we are, there is nothing like a smile and a hug. We all look to others to brighten our day, and what better way to do it than by spreading the beautiful message of an embrace?

VIRTUAL WORLDS

There are also virtual worlds on the internet like Second Life for adults or Club Penguin for children. In both of those worlds you are playing a game with your avatar, and in the case of both platforms, you can customize your world to the last detail. In the case of Second Life, you can create the gesture of a hug and build your own sign, exactly as you would in real life. As a culture we spend more and more time on these platforms. On Second Life, people are buying and selling virtual clothes, and giving concerts and making real money from it. People are gathering avatars for discussions and events. It is possible that on Second Life or other similar platforms, your avatar could literally be holding up a Free Hugs sign and giving away hugs to anyone that came up to you! Is that as real or as pleasurable as the physical hugs on a street corner? Perhaps it is if you spend a lot of time on those sites.

Events can be created. As we were saying, you could even hold up signs with other friends. These relationships could turn into real physical ones, and all of the people that you were giving away hugs with could do it in your neighborhood in real life. The world that could be considered imaginary can turn very real, and the money you might raise in that manner could also be very real.

The advantage of using social media platforms is that they can enable you to experiment easily and then form groups of people that can discuss ideas that are taken out to the physical world. This type of inter-action is happening more and more, so why not use them to make your life richer with more friends than you actually get to meet? As artists, we are always meeting people through Google Plus, Twitter, and other platforms. We not only meet real people, but we meet interesting people who we can get to know a bit before planning on a cafe or other place to meet. In fact, we have found social media to be one of the greatest tools in our career as artists.

The digital revolution has already transformed parts of the world with real revolutions, with people uniting behind a common cause to do great and unforgettable things. And just as Amma started with simple charitable tasks for her neighbors, and Juan Mann with the desire for human comfort, you can reach out to every part of the world with just one good intention.

Tree Huggers

A stricken tree, a living thing, so beautiful, so dignified, so admirable in its potential longevity, is, next to man, perhaps the most touching of wounded objects.

—Edna Ferber

CHAPTER SEVEN

Tree Huggers

THE TERM "TREE HUGGERS" can be used in a derogatory way to describe environmentalists or those opposed to cutting down trees and deforestation. The social movement of hugging trees to literally stop the machines and axes from cutting them down is thought to have started in the 1970s, but there is an earlier example, called the Chipko movement or Chipo Andolan. It is a Hindi term that literally means "to stick," and like the modern tree huggers, the people who practiced it used non-violent methods of resistance that were encouraged by Ghandi to stop trees from being cut down.

On March 26th, 1974, as more people began to become aware of deforestation, a group of peasant women in Reni village, Hemwalghati, in Chamoli district, Uttarakhand, India, began a protest to stop the removal of trees by the state. Their protests inspired hundreds of people to do the same, and it ushered in a new era of sensitivity to the policies of deforestation, which spread all over India. As part of the global consciousness that was growing at that time, it quickly spread to countries all over the world. Those women were recalling another landmark historical event. In 1730, a group from India called the Bishnois, who have origins in the fifteenth century and carry out a religious mission to protect animal and plant life, protested as well. When the local ruler sent loggers to cut the trees, Amrita Devi, their leader, said she would offer her head if it would save one tree. So she went forward with her belief and the loggers cut her head off with an axe. Her last words were, "If a tree is saved even at the cost of one's head, it's worth it." Three girls followed her and met the same fate.

The Bishnois began gathering to decide the next steps, and many elders came from the community to offer their lives while holding trees. They were all killed by axes, and the local ruler mocked them, calling out that the old protesters were worthless. Then young men and women, often with families, offered their heads as well, and it is said that even children were killed while embracing trees. As this went on, chaos ensued, and the people cutting the trees and slaughtering hundreds of Bishnois began to worry that the killings were not having the desired effect. The group of tree-cutters and their leader left, and told the Maharaja what happened. The deaths stopped immediately. In the end, there were 363 martyrs.

The ruler of Jodhpur, Maharaja Abhay Singh, apologized for the mistake committed by his officials and issued a royal decree, engraved on a copper plate ordering the following:

➤ ◄

All cutting of green trees and hunting of animals within the revenue boundaries of Bishnoi villages is strictly prohibited.

➤ ◄

It was also ordered that if by mistake any individual violated this order, he would be prosecuted by state and a severe penalty imposed. Even members of the ruling family did not shoot animals in or even near the Bishnois' village.

This extraordinary story is considered the seed of the modern movement that began in 1974 and continues to this day. The anniversary of the massacre is celebrated every year in the Bishnois' village, and it has become a tourist attraction as well because of that. The Bishnois will still sacrifice their lives to protect animals that are being poached in the area, but now, people who are caught poaching animals on their land can be arrested and jailed.

The modern movement in the United States got great attention when the radical group Earth First began organizing what are now viewed as publicity stunts, such as building tree houses, or platforms in trees. The members would stay in the trees for as long as possible, and it brought worldwide publicity to their efforts. Earth First believes that the current movements to preserve wilderness are conservative and not doing nearly enough, and continue to create groups in other countries building on the efforts.

The website www.treehugger.com is a place that teaches readers how to "go green." To be green has many meanings, from getting the right hybrid car to recycling, and all other forms of what it means to do your best to be sensitive and caring to our planet. It is an example of how the term has an expanded definition now. It has become a catch-all phrase for people who are sensitive to environmental concerns. Though it is often used to make light of the concerns of environmentalists, if you think about the martyrs in India who continue to inspire to this day, maybe you will be proud to be tree hugger.

There are others who have used the term to define their own work. And one example is the TreeHugger Project, where Wiktor Szostalo and Agnieszka Gradzik create environmental art pieces that are literal tree huggers. Their sculptures are twigs, vines, sticks, and branches woven together and entwined to create wicker people that wrap their arms around tree trunks. What could be simpler? Their projects are mainly St. Louis–based, but their work has also taken Gradzik and Szostalo to Hebden Bridge in England. The duo's mission is to rediscover their relationship with nature while encouraging others to think about their own attitudes toward the surrounding world.

The Free Hugs movement has been largely about hugging people, but why not make videos of you hugging trees and animals? Just like the Bishnois martyrs in India, you are saying that animals and trees should be considered worthy of your passion and protection. And by hugging the tree or animal, you are illustrating an ancient form of courage. People have often called the movement naïve, but as long as you keep your role in perspective, and devote your passion to it, you can do your little bit to further the environmental cause. Do your research, lobby your representatives, and, if you're feeling generous with the world, go out and hug a tree.

CHAPTER EIGHT

Hugs in the News

Men greet each other with a sock on the arm, women with a hug, and the hug wears better in the long run.
　　　　　　　　—Edward Hoagland

Chapter Eight

Hugs in the News

MEN LIKE HUGS MORE THAN WOMEN?

A SURVEY IN INDIA OF around one hundred couples concluded that men seemed to want hugs and cuddling more than women, and that for men, hugs made them happier in their relationships. Psychologists have weighed in on why this is the case, but with varying theories. Since men are no longer dominant in the household, and times have changed about expressing sensitivity, it might be that men can now feel more comfortable expressing affection.

HUGGING SCHOOLCHILDREN

In California, schoolteachers, especially men, are wary of hugging children, because it could be misconstrued as molestation. Many teachers are careful, but others say it is something to work around. Some teachers give a sideways hug, or a shoulder hug, to have as little contact as possible. It has been suggested that if a child approaches a teacher for a hug they give them a high-five instead. Of course, this all seems very sad, because when a child wants a hug for comfort, and embraces the teacher, it is a sign of trust and also need. Where the line is drawn is up to the individual teacher, but the main rule now is not to ever be alone with a student. All of these new rules about hugs in the classroom have arisen out of suits against the school for inappropriate touching. Teachers are told to refrain when possible from ever touching a student.

THE RECORD FOR GIVING OUT THE MOST HUGS

On February 14th, 2010, 7,777 hugs were given out by Jeff Ondash. He is also the record-holder for the most hugs given out in one hour, according to the

Guinness Book of World Records. In just one hour, he gave out 1,205 hugs!

HUGGING AND INTIMACY

A recent report says that couples who hug and cuddle more often are likely to be happier together. That means cuddling at night while sleeping and also on the couch while watching television. While the common belief is that a lack of sex can drive couples apart, it seems that intimacy is what is needed even more, and the form of a hug can work very well.

When a couple is on a couch hugging or cuddling, they are also talking and communicating their emotions. During sex, that is not always the case, but as part of being close to one another, a hug can foster conversation about mutual feelings and improve communication on the deepest levels. If sex is the only form of intimacy in a relationship, then emotional issues may never be discussed, while hugs and touching produce oxytocin, the chemical that not only makes you feel good, but makes you want more of the same.

GLOBAL HUG YOUR KIDS DAY!

On July 16th, the Hug Your Kids Foundation promotes the idea that if you have children, you should hug them more. Hugging is an important emotional support for children. Of course, you are encouraged to hug them every single day, not just once a year! On their site they have a thirty-day hug challenge, which is a calendar you print out and check off every time you hug your child or someone else.

MICHELLE OBAMA AND HUGS

Hugs have been used in political circles as a visual means to communicate friendship between leaders and between countries. When Michelle Obama, the First Lady, took a trip to Africa in 2011 she was received very warmly. One thing people didn't expect was for her to be hugging children and others she met. Some were reduced to tears at the unusual outreach and intimacy of a political figure as important as she is. As an advocate for her husband's policies, those gestures won her a lot of supporters.

When Michelle Obama welcomed G20 leaders in Pittsburgh, she gave a hug to all the major leaders of countries, but not to Silvio Berlusconi, the prime minister of Italy. In the image taken that day, he seemed clearly miffed that she offered him a handshake! The hug in this case is a powerful gesture, and the lack of one a clear statement.

Hugs and Spirituality

You can't give a hug without getting a
hug.

—Jacques-Benigne Bossuet

CHAPTER NINE

Hugs and Spirituality

DEVELOP YOUR OWN PRACTICE of spirituality on your own terms as a way to engage the world, a way to enlightenment, or a way to peace of mind.

THE SPIRITUALITY OF FREE HUGS

The beginning of any spiritual practice is the most fun, because it is new, different, and carries the hope of making you happier or more fulfilled. You can be enthusiastic and dedicated without having put in your first day! It is about the possibility of something greater for you in the future. There is always that possibility that something incredible will happen to you, that one day, unexpectedly, something will really click into place and you will be spending almost all of your time doing what you love. A successful artist is an example of that, but it could be any profession at all. And it could also be just an adjustment in your schedule. For example, today we are writing early in the morning, and as authors, parents, and artists, our time is heavily scheduled. We just decided that starting tomorrow we will rise earlier, write from about 6 a.m. to 8 a.m., then take our son to school, and then home and work and other things. Getting two more hours out of our day is very important to us, and even inspiring. Though we have not even started that schedule yet, which will help to complete this book, we are excited about the idea of it. It has potential to help us become more productive, and the thought does not cause panic, it creates ease, because we are more organized.

Having said that, the beginning of a new adventure, like turning Free Hugs into your new religion or spiritual practice, can be inspiring before you even begin. If that is where you are now, thinking about it, well, good for you; no matter what happens next, you are about to be inspired, because it is an easy and generous path.

STEP ONE: YOUR MATERIALS

To begin, you have to gather a few materials that are special to you. You might already have them. A small object like a marble or a cup or a photograph that makes you smile or makes you happy for any reason. Make a little tiny sign that says FREE HUGS. Select one to three objects like that. Take your time, then go to the next step.

STEP TWO: HONOR YOURSELF

Gather your elements of happiness and put them on a shelf or in some protected place like an altar. We are using the word altar because that is what you are making. You can also consider it a wishing well, or a Happy Spot, or whatever word you are comfortable with. It is a monument to peace and happiness and having a good day. It is the core of your new spiritual practice.

STEP THREE: START WORSHIPPING!

Now it's time to pray! We are not religious believers in the traditional sense in any way, but it can't hurt to pray a little. It is very similar to meditation, really. Your first act in this scenario is to go to the place where your elements are gathered. Stand or sit for thirty seconds only, no more or less. In those thirty seconds you can either count to thirty slowly, or think about the content of the elements in front of you. Think about the memories associated with them. Smile. If you are not smiling at this point, then something is wrong. It's also okay to force yourself to smile, that works too. The idea is that you are making an effort to focus on memories that make you happy and inspire you.

STEP FOUR: TAKE ACTION!

An action of some kind is next, one that seems in line with your smile that you generated in steps two and three. We suggest you begin by hugging yourself with a big embrace by stretching each one of your arms around your back. No matter how awkward this initially feels, enjoy it for at least ten seconds. Other actions could be hugging someone else, or a tree, or just calling or writing a friend and giving them the equivalent of a hug, by sharing a bit of enthusiasm and happiness with them.

STEP FIVE: WRITE TO US!

Do this every day for a week, for five minutes or less, and write us a letter, and send a picture of your altar, and you will get your FREE HUGS membership card with more tips on passing out good vibes wherever you go.

STEP SIX: START CHANGING THE WORLD!

Change the actions you do each day. One day it could just be smiling at someone, and making them smile in return. On another day it could giving out free hugs in your neighborhood or nearby city. Hugs are very powerful and for us, they are the most potent and direct way to express kindness.

Those are the six steps to get going with your practice. We do this every day and it has made our lives noticeably brighter by forcing us to focus on something happy to begin our day (we do it in the mornings). It also has made us both more aware that everyday acts and small gestures can improve the quality of life for all of us.

MAKE A COMMITMENT

If you like this process, and if you are also out there giving out hugs, part of doing this is making a commitment to yourself. That will also give you a certain type of euphoric reaction to the possibility of doing something at length that is good for you. Consider committing yourself for a year. It could be less, but a year is a good amount of time, and will bear real fruit in terms of your outlook on life. Consider it a one-year experiment with being kinder and giving out more hugs.

You may want to go out with a Free Hugs sign, and you may not. Some people can do that and for others, that isn't the path. No matter which you choose, this book and this particular chapter is about actions that you can decide to commit yourself to or not. By reading this far, you have already made a statement to yourself about the kind of content you are interested in. Find a way to use that passion. Perhaps it is following the steps outlined.

CHANGE

We are strong believers that change is good! If one thing isn't working, try something else. After you assemble your altar elements, maybe one of them bothers you, so change it.

Or perhaps there is a spot in your neighborhood where you are giving out hugs that isn't working, so change it. Pick another spot outside your neighborhood.

Even if you are committing to a year of following the Free Hugs practice, you can change how that is expressed for you. If you only hugged yourself every day for a year, and wrote about it, that could be your practice as well.

You are an innovator, a seeker, and you will customize your way so it will be the easiest and the most fun, and be what you are driven to do.

USE YOUR OTHER PRACTICES

Perhaps you practice yoga, or you're a Christian, Buddhist, Muslim, or Jew, and you observe regular holidays and a prayer schedule, or a similar practice. Can this fit in with all of those, and if so, how?

The idea of fitting in your Free Hugs practice is like fitting in an extra piece of dessert, even if you are full. Yes, you could replace what you are doing with this practice, but it is also easy enough to fit into your daily routine as an extra.

SUPPORT

As the authors of this book, we are also here to help. So send us an email if you have a question, and we will send you our support kit, which includes a FREE HUGS sign you can print out as well as more information to keep you updated and involved in everything Free Hugs! The movement is also all around the world. There are countless resources in every country and online. Reach out and connect!

We can be reached at www.theartofhugging.com.

Change the World— One Hug at a Time

A hug is the shortest distance between friends.

—Anonymous

Chapter Ten

Change the World—One Hug at a Time

ERE IS A CALL to action to start your own Hug movement or create something different to help the world directly.

Maybe at one time or another you have asked yourself what your purpose is on this earth or wondered if there is something you can do to feel more fulfilled here. We all do, and there is something for all of us, for sure. But if you haven't found that one passion yet, there are many things you can do in the meantime.

There is an idea that in thirty days, you can try something different and see if it works, see if it sticks. One well-known example is National Novel Writing Month. Every year, people from around the world commit to the tremendous task of writing a complete novel in just thirty days. The way it is done is that you break it up into small segments, such as 1,600 words a day. You promise yourself that you will not go to sleep unless you write those words every day. We know a friend that does this every year, spilling out 50,000 words right before the holidays. She doesn't publish the novel; she could, but that isn't the point. The idea is to prove to yourself that it is possible and that you can change your life in small increments.

Why not try to give a hug a day for thirty days? It's certainly easier than writing a novel. You can download a calendar from us, and decide that you will give out a hug once a day for thirty days. If you have a child, you could commit to hugging your child, or your lover, or your mother, or yourself! Thirty days seems to be the time it takes to change a habit, so why not try it? Make it easy, not monumental. Pick something that you could easily achieve to try out the system.

We use this system regularly when we want to make a change of some kind. The reason it is so attractive to us is because change is seen rapidly, and that is so satisfying. We are all used to certain habits, and some of those habits we are not even aware of,

like how affectionate we are with other people. As a couple, we are an American and native Spaniard. In Spain, there is a more affectionate culture, whereas in America it is a bit colder. These are not innate desires or directed efforts; they are cultural conditions we have grown up in. In Europe, there is much more touching between people, even those who do not

know each other. In Spain, when you are introduced to someone for the first time, it is not uncommon to kiss them on the cheek. In the streets and in public, you see couples casually caressing and being affectionate. In America, however, we do not see the same kind of affection shown publicly. This is not a comment on which culture is better or worse, just an observation. As a couple, we are always working on this, but one thing that got us further was using the thirty-day method to adjust our behavior. To touch more, to be more affectionate, is a physical activity that you can measure.

Whether you brighten the day of a close friend or spark a movement that spills out across the web, a simple gesture and some dedication can start you on the road to something huge.

The Do-It-Yourself Guide

Millions and millions of years would still not give me half enough time to describe that tiny instant of all eternity when you put your arms around me and I put my arms around you.

—Jacques Prévert

CHAPTER ELEVEN

The Do-It-Yourself Guide

THIS IS THE FUN part: go out and give out free hugs! There are several things to keep in mind while doing this, so before you go, here are some tips, as well as our experience.

When we first began giving hugs on the open street instead of our storefront on 10th Street, it took some bravery. As we stepped out the door, looking for a place to give hugs, we were carrying this big sign, and weren't sure whether to hide it or not until we found our spot. Finally we arrived on a corner. It was 9th Street and 2nd Avenue, and we held up our sign. Honestly, it takes some guts to do this. You are exposing yourself to the public in a way that you never have before. We didn't say a word, just held up our sign looking around to see who would come by. It was a busy afternoon in New York City, and there were a lot of people in the street. We started to say "free hugs" every now and then, but still nothing. As you stand there, you start to look in people's faces as they walk by, and imagine that they will come forward, but they don't. Initially it feels like so many rejections!

But then a person comes forward with open arms, and you give and receive a hug. Suddenly we both felt energized again. That is really the key, to be brave enough to wait, and suddenly you will get a hug and it will fill you with excitement. It will give you the energy to wait for another. We stayed out for about two hours that first day, and it was like having two cups of coffee. It was thrilling—it felt almost magical, and we were proud. That first bit of being scared was important to feel, because once we got over that, we felt better because we had done something we didn't realize we could do.

YOU ARE READY

Now that you are ready to at least think about giving out free hugs, here are the steps you can take to do it.

FIND YOUR SIGN

To begin with, make a sign that says Free Hugs. You can use paper, but sometimes it folds in the wind and can be hard to manage. We go to the art supply store and get a piece of foam core, which is a white, cardboard-like material that is often used in picture frames as backing for the artwork. With a permanent marker, write your big letters that say Free Hugs. We also print out signs that we just pick up from our local printer. You can also print out a sign by going to our website, www.theartofhugging.com, and clicking on the "hugs" link. Simple, right?

MULTIPLY

You can keep making signs for an event of hugs. If you need 100 signs or more, you can get a local printer to do all of it for you. If you have a modest budget, a local printer can make signs cheaply in a variety of ways, and even put sticks on them if you want them too! The more people that are holding signs, the better! In a group, everyone feels more confident about what they are doing, and you are never alone, waiting for a hug. Also, in a group there is a great sense of celebration, of camaraderie, and it spreads to everyone coming near it. When a group gathers to give out free hugs, it is also a sign of hope and beauty, that the human spirit is so generous and that life can be poetic as well as simple.

GROUP TIPS, GENERAL MARKETING

If you are assembling a group, Facebook, Google Plus, and Twitter can all be useful in gathering a crowd. Once you have done a group hug video or taken pictures of the activities, post them on a blog like Tumblr, or another sharing site.

If you want to raise money for a cause or a project this way, here are a few tips, as well as a plan for your school, charity, or organization.

♥ Use the Web

Consider using a site like www.kickstarter .com to tell the world what you are doing (giving out hugs) and what you are raising money for. Make a video, have fun, be passionate, but most important of all, spread the word using social media and networking platforms like Twitter, YouTube, Google Plus, and Facebook.

♥ Spread the Word

Like anything that succeeds, the world must know all about it, and you have to find a way to share with the world your plans and intentions. In this case, you also have to get them involved by becoming supporters of hugs or at least spreading the word about your goals. If you are using Twitter, for example, tell people whenever you are going out to give out hugs, and post pictures of it when you can. If you want to be more organized and raise money regularly or just do it for fun, then plan in advance.

Set up dates and times and places where you will be next, and tell everyone when it will start or how it will work. Be specific. If you have signs made already, tell your followers, and if it will last two hours, or more or less, make sure everyone is in the loop on that, too.

GET OUT ONTO THE STREET

When you are ready, with your plan in place, take your sign and maybe a friend or two (or more!) and find a place that is busy and has a lot of people walking by. That could be a college campus, a local park, or anywhere you can think of where there will be a lot of people walking by. Pick a time of day when you know it will be busy, like lunch hour. Have a friend with a camera to take pictures and videos. A video is important because you can see all the smiles and fun it creates!

When you find your spot, just hold up your sign and wait. You can smile or wave at people, but ultimately you have to wait until they come to you. Don't hug someone who isn't ready—the beauty of free hugs is that they come to you! If you have brought a friend, you can take turns holding the sign.

One of the most important things is to be brave and patient. The hardest part of all this is standing out there with your sign, waiting. Some people will look, but not ask for a hug, and even if you are just standing around for a minute or so, it will be a new experience, so be patient, and be brave; people will come to you!

DOCUMENTATION

If you are going to do this more than once, you should write a press release and send it out to your local newspapers, television stations, and blogs, and they will come! If you want help writing a press release, we have one written for you already, and you can download it from our website.

It is important to let the press know, not because it's fun to have your picture in the paper and on the news, but because it will encourage other people to do it, and just reading about it or seeing it on TV will make people happy! If you make a video, put it on YouTube and send us a link. If you have a blog, send it to us, and we will give you a link on our site. It is important to have some good photographs of your event on your blog or website and also available to press for printing. Connect with us! We want to help you spread the word about your movement.

RAISE MONEY FOR CHARITY

Raising money for a local charity or a school project? Why not use hugs? It is more environmentally sustainable than cookies! All cynical comments aside, hugs are the ultimate renewable resource. Almost anyone can participate! All you need to do is set up a group to organize it with you, and follow these steps.

♥ Put a Team Together

Gather a committee of at least three people to do this—if you want this to really grow, get together with one or two friends and assign tasks and roles. Someone takes care of regular postings to the blog, and another person takes care of donations, and a third person handles where, when, and how and organizes the regular meetings between the three or more. Listen to each other carefully. Everyone wants to do this for different reasons, for different motivations, so be sensitive to everyone's interests and ideas. This is a collaborative process and must be handled accordingly. If everyone is able to commit to their assigned roles, you'll have a smoother road ahead.

♥ The Catchy Name and the Financial Goal

Name your project, for example, "Hugs for New Baseballs," and pick a financial goal, such as $1,000.

Choosing a goal for your fundraising is important, because when the goal is reached, it is time to celebrate and thank all of those who supported it. Remember, you can always move beyond your goal, but reaching it should be your first priority. By marking a goal, there is an end, and it is also a way of saying the dream has been achieved, and that is what the donors and your friends want to hear!

♥ Make Your Case

You can choose whatever amount you want, from ten cents a hug to a dollar a hug. Print out a form (which you can also download on our site), that has lines and columns for names, emails, and dollar amounts. Then you and anyone who wants to raise money either goes door to door in your neighborhood, or asks by email. What you say is that you are giving out hugs to raise money for, say, new baseballs for your school, and you are asking someone to sponsor you at ten cents a hug. Then the person you are asking says, "How do I know you have given out the hugs?" You can tell them that a video will be made and posted online, and they can see you giving out hugs. They can choose a maximum amount, but essentially they are pledging to give you a certain amount for every hug you give. After you give the hugs, you can collect the money pledged based on how many hugs you gave away. Much easier than wrapping paper, right?

For example, let's say you and your friends will give out a hug on video for every dollar donated. So for $10,000, you will see a video with many hugs given out, 10,000 in fact! That is the evidence that their money has not only given out a hug, but has also helped a cause of your choice. Once you have reached your goal and made a video, make another press release announcing your success!

You can also ask a local business to pledge a certain amount toward a goal with a maximum donation, say $100. You can tell the business that they will be credited as having supported 100 local hugs, which will certainly bring them attention and goodwill!

♥ Document!

Be sure to start a blog to record the hugs you have given out, and, if you are raising money, record how much is given each day or week towards your goal. Having a record of what you're doing helps establish credibility if you want to do another project. Your donors can see exactly what they've contributed to, and your blog will represent another bright space for people to discover.

♥ Keep Track

Keep careful track of the finances and report your taxes according to the law! Guidelines for charitable donations can easily be found online. The worst-case scenario would be to have a successful campaign be derailed by the details of paperwork. Keep on top of your records and consult someone who can help you make sure you're doing everything right. All of your donations should be accounted for.

We welcome you to visit our website at www.theartofhugging.com to download more information, sample press releases that you can tailor to your own needs, and just to take a look around. As you can see, starting a movement can be as simple as getting a few passionate friends together. We can't wait to see what you'll do!

Afterword

NOW YOU ARE READY to go out and give a hug to your friends, your lover, your husband, your wife, your child, or the general public. Be bold, be brave, and know that many have walked in your footsteps and that soon you will receive the same support and payback they did. We were excited to make sure this book was one you could carry around with you, and hope that it will help and inspire you as you go on your journey. You will find that the world not only wants to get a hug from you, it wants to give you one as well!

About the Authors

BRAINARD AND DELIA CAREY are conceptual artists who have built their lives on hopes and dreams. That notion might seem quaint or cliché, but in this case, it's true. As artists, sometimes that dream might be a little crazy, like washing feet and giving out hugs, but in their case, it worked. From humble beginnings, they built their career on ideas that might take flight, and this book is one of them. Their art work has been displayed at the Whitney Biennial, at PS1/MoMA, and the Reina Sofia. They are always working on new dreams through their collaborative, Praxis. They enjoy traveling between homes in New York City and New Haven, Connecticut. Their son Shiva is also a dreamer.